Through It All - TRUST
When it seems your world is crumbling

A Bible Study Companion to Rock Solid Trust

VIRGINIA GROUNDS

All rights reserved. No part of this book may be used or reproduced by any means, graphic, electronic, or mechanical, including photocopying or by any information storage retrieval system without the written permission of the author except in the case of brief quotations embodied in critical articles and reviews.

This book is a work of non-fiction and a study guide.

Images used in cover design are models, and such images are being used for illustrative purposes only. Stock imagery Getty Images.

Scripture quotations marked (NIV) are taken from the Holy Bible, New International Version, copyright 1973, 1978, 1984, 2011 by Biblica, Ins. Used by permission of Zondervan. All rights reserved worldwide. www.zondervan.com. The "NIV" and "New International Version" are trademarks registered in the United States Patent and Trademark Office by Biblica, Inc.

Scripture quotations marked HCSB, are taken from the Holman Christian Standard Bible, copyright 1999, 2000, 2002, 2003, 2009 by Holman Bible Publishers. Used by permission. HCSB is a federally registered trademark of Holman Bible Publishers.

Scripture quotations taken from the New American Standard Bible (NASB), copyright 1960, 1962, 1963, 1968, 1971, 1972, 1973, 1975, 1977, 1995 by the Lockman Foundation used by permission. www.lockman.org.

Scripture taken from the New King James Version, copyright 1982 by Thomas Nelson. Used by permission. All rights reserved.

Cover Photo: Gettyimages.com

About the Author and Contact Information, Page 83

Copyright © 2018 Virginia Grounds

All rights reserved.

ISBN-10: 1983867918
ISBN-13: 978-1983867910

*The instruction of the LORD is perfect,
renewing one's life;
The testimony of the LORD is trustworthy,
Making the inexperienced wise*

Psalm 19:7 (HCSB)

Table of Contents

1	**Introduction**	1
	• Message Notes	4
2	**Week One – Solid Trust**	5
	• Day 1 – One and Only	
	• Day 2 – God The Rock	
	• Day 3 – The Rock or a rock	
	• Day 4 – Ungodly Celebration	
	• Day 5 – What Are Idols	
	• Message Notes	24
3	**Week Two – Trusting When Exhausted**	25
	• Day 1 – David's Exhaustion	
	• Day 2 – Crying Out	
	• Day 3 – David's Song	
	• Day 4 – Help is from the LORD	
	• Day 5 – According to His Word	
	• Message Notes	41
4	**Week Three – Trusting When Threatened**	43
	• Day 1 – Identifying the Threat	
	• Day 2 – Committing to the LORD	
	• Day 3 – God's Response	
	• Day 4 – Song of Obedience	
	• Day 5 – Blessings of Doing What is Right	
	• Message Notes	62
5	**Week Four – Trusting When Suffering**	63
	• Day 1 – Spiritual Rock	
	• Day 2 – Through It All	
	• Day 3 – Song of Salvation	
	• Day 4 – Tools for Solid Trust	
	• Day 5 – Desired Result	
	• Message Notes	82

Through it All - TRUST

Through It All - TRUST?

*"Trust in the LORD forever, for in God the Lord,
we have an everlasting Rock."*
Isaiah 26:4

Introduction:

Do you feel as if life has thrown you a curveball? Do you look around you and wonder how in the world there is so much disrespect, violence and pain today? The answer is simple, but hard. We live in a fallen world. It hasn't been so long ago that knowing this and seeing results of it were two different things. But today, we see evidence of a fallen world *every* day.

Because of what we see and hear on the news and social media, fear of the future and not trusting that anything can be different than it is now is an emotion taking root in many hearts. This fear weakens our ability to trust others, and especially weakens our faith and trust in God.

Who can you trust in this fallen world? How do you build a deeper trust in God, a trust that does not falter, no matter what happens?
- By planting the seeds of truth from His word deep into your heart and mind.
- By looking at who God is in scripture.
- By looking at how His character and identity apply to your own life.
- By praying His word back to Him in praise and thanksgiving.

As I have taught and listened to women and heard their stories of living in this ever-changing society, a common thread has emerged. That is a lack of trust, or shattered trust, from circumstances beyond their control. Why? As the old saying goes, *the times, they are a-changing*. We are seeing more violence on the news every day. We are hearing about things that were once unmentionable, but are now put on the screen before us for all to see, and for our children to ask questions about. Young people are being kidnapped and sold into slavery. Time after time, we hear of people who have proven to be untrustworthy.

Perhaps your trust has faltered because of a situation in one of those areas. If so, I have good news for you. There is One who does not change, who is faithful and trustworthy. He is the One that is rock solid. You can trust God for the future. He already has a plan for you. This study is written for the purpose of directing your attention to the reasons why you can trust Him. It is written to help you understand that when everything around you is crumbling, and doubts enter your mind, The Rock of our salvation will never shatter. He will never crumble under the weight of your burdens and your doubts. He is strong enough to carry you through whatever is troubling to you, and He will do it.

In traveling to Haiti and El Salvador on mission in the past, I have seen on the faces of women the helplessness that comes from their mistreatment. But I have also seen the hope they have in God because their trust in Him is solid. If these women from around the world who have suffered so much can trust God, then surely we can build a stronger faith and trust in Him ourselves.

Let's commit to seeking Him in a new and fresh way as we look at the lives of Moses, David and Jehoshaphat, three great men of the Bible who trusted God when others did not, who trusted when exhausted from fighting the same old battles and when overwhelmed by circumstances.

My prayer as I write this study is that God will use it to remove any doubts you may have about trusting Him and fill your heart with a song of praise as you trust Him in every situation. You can trust in the love of God because He is bigger and stronger and more than you can ever imagine, and yet, He loves you. You can trust that!

Through it All - TRUST

Trusting in God's Love

Higher than the heavens
Deeper than the sea
Wider than the earth is round
That's Your love for me.

More than any person
More than earthly wealth
More than silver or gold,
Precious jewels or anything else

That's how much You love me
That's how much You care
That's a love I cannot explain
Yet, of which, I am very aware.

So thank You LORD for loving me
Even knowing mistakes I've made
Thank you for grace and forgiveness
And the life-changing sacrifice you made.

Your love is amazing
It's so high and deep and wide.
How can I not but trust you
Knowing you are always by my side.

Virginia -

Message Notes

Week One – Day One

One and Only

He is the Rock, His works are perfect and all His ways are just. A faithful god who does no wrong, upright and just is He.
Deuteronomy 32:4 (NIV)

Trust, what does it mean to you? Does it come easily, or do you have a difficult time trusting? Without trust, it is difficult to move forward in life with confidence that your needs will be met. The meaning of the word trust is "lean on, rely upon, have confidence in". Without trust, you may lean and find yourself falling with nothing, or no one, to hold you up. You may rely on people who are not trustworthy, or place your confidence in things that do not satisfy and then wonder why you feel so discontent and insecure.

A life lived without trusting in God is an empty life without hope for the future, without the only source of strength that can walk with you through the valleys of life to the goodness on the other side.

And so, do you have a lack of confidence? If so, the root may be fear that stems from a lack of trust. Please begin this study with prayer asking God to show you and teach you how to be confident by learning how to trust Him more.

Trust Building Reminders

> **Trust Building Reminders**

Throughout the study, I want you to look at the scripture you read from four different ways. It is a method of studying the Bible using the acrostic **READ**. That is, **read, example or exhortation, application, direction**. If you will think in terms of these four things as you study, I believe this method will enhance your insight and understanding.

And so, I want to stop here for a moment and explain it. But first, read Deuteronomy 32:4. I will use this verse to explain the study method.

First, **READ** the verse. These are the facts - the truths of scripture – God is THE ROCK, His work is perfect, His ways are just, He is faithful, righteous and upright.

The EXAMPLE or EXHORTATION is to those whom Moses was speaking. What example did he use that they could relate with, or what exhortation did he give? The example for them is the identity of God in this passage as the one and only God and a description of His character.

The APPLICATION is for you the reader to ask the question, **how does this apply to me personally?** *God the rock is strong, I can lean on Him. He will treat me fairly, always doing what is just for me. Because He is faithful, I can trust Him with my life and needs. He is righteous; there is no wrong in Him so I can know that whatever He does in my life is for my best. And through Him, I can stand rock solid in my faith.*

And then the DIRECTION which includes prayer. This is where you look at the scripture, in this case the identity of God, and then you pray asking for direction according to the scripture and application for you. Are you going in the right direction or is change needed. Possibly something like this: *"God my Rock, thank you for who you are in my life. Thank you for showing me that I can trust you confident that you always know what is best for me. Help me to accept your wisdom and purpose in my life. Lead me on the path of righteousness and when I stumble, set my feet upon the solid Rock of Christ Jesus. I am committing anew to you to stand strong and firm in my faith trusting in you. Amen"*

> **Trust Building Reminders**

1. This week, you will read through Deuteronomy 32 and see God's message to Israel through His servant, Moses. Read verses 1-2. What words of action do you see in verse 1?

2. What are the people to hear? See also 31:30.

3. From verse 2, name the ways Moses is asking that his teaching fall on the people.

    a. Fall like _____
    b. Descend like _____
    c. Like _____
    d. Like _____

Trust Building Reminders

4. What happens when rain falls on new grass and tender plants?

5. Read Hosea 6:3. What is the promise of God when we press on to acknowledge Him?

6. Moses asked for it; God promised it. James 4:8 says *"Draw near to God and He will draw near to you."* And so, if you hear what God teaches through His word, if you come to Him and acknowledge who He is in your life, what trust building truth did you read that gives you assurance?

7. Studying the Bible is about new life, growth and relationship. If you want to be able to trust God more, to experience His strength, to have **greater** confidence, you need to

Through it All - TRUST

read His word, pay attention to what it says and then act upon it.

APPLICATION - Based on what you have studied today, what action do you need to take in order to build your trust? Also read Hebrews 10:22 and list the four conditions for drawing near to God. Write these in your reminder box.

In order to trust, you must have faith. Draw near to God in prayer. Ask God to reveal any weak areas in your ability to trust so you will be aware of what action you need to take, if any, to build a greater confidence.

Trust Building Reminders

Trust Building Reminders

Week One - Day 2

God is The Rock

Continue your reading of Deuteronomy 32. Read verses 3-4. Moses said *"I will proclaim the name of the LORD. Oh, praise the greatness of our God!"*

1. What name did Moses call God in verse 4?

2. What is the preposition before the name and what does it mean?

APPLICATION: And so, by identifying God as The Rock, what does that say to you personally? (Remember, this is the application portion of READ) Use the space in the Trust Building Reminders box.

3. How is God described? List the descriptive phrases in verse 4.

4. Without looking back at Day One, explain how these phrases apply to you.

The word "perfect" in the Hebrew is "Tamlym. It is the divine standard which man must attain. He must try to meet all the requirements of God's law." The word perfect means, *integrity, entire, complete, without blemish, sincere, undefiled and upright*.

God created His works perfect, but sin entered in through Adam. Therefore, we are not born perfect, but born into sin. And so, if we do not enter in to the perfection that is only found in Jesus, our lives are spent striving for a perfection we will never achieve apart from Christ.

Are you a perfectionist? Are you a person who wants everything as you want it and feel you are the only one who can make it that way? I know what I am talking about because I used to be that way. A perfectionist is never satisfied with the end result and keeps trying to make it, whatever "it" is, better until they are dragged kicking and screaming from the "it" they are trying to perfect. Well, maybe not literally, but in their mind they are probably kicking and screaming.

I learned that true perfection will never be achieved until we are in our glorified bodies with Christ. Life is so much easier when I am more flexible and accepting of what is rather than what is not. I learned that trusting my ability to achieve perfection was an indication that I was not trusting God in that area of my life.

Trust Building Reminders

Trust Building Reminders

5. Read what Hebrews 7:11, 18-22 say about perfection, the law and the new covenant. Write your insights below.

6. God has begun a work of perfection in you, but when will that perfection be complete? Read Philippians 1:6.

7. Based on this verse, can you achieve perfection in your life now?

8. What are you to do until the day of Christ according to verses 9-10?

9. And how are you able to accomplish those actions? See verse 11

Remember, part of the definition of perfect is sincere and blameless. The works of God *The* Rock are perfect. He wants you, whom He created, to strive toward sincerity and moral action. You are able because He is righteous and is working His righteousness in you. Can you trust what He has written? Read Psalm 19:7-9 to find out and write your observations.

Ask God to show you areas of your life where you are not flexible and to help you let go. Let Him take control. Acknowledge that He is Sovereign.

Trust Building Reminders

God will bring this about in His own time. He is the blessed and only sovereign, the King of kings, and the Lord of lords...

1 Timothy 6:15 (HCSB)

Trust Building Reminders

Week One – Day 3

<u>The</u> Rock or a rock?

Today's reading is longer than usual, but will help you in the days to come. Read Deuteronomy 32:3-43.

1. Make a note of each time the word "Rock" and the word "rock" are mentioned. List the verse references as well.
a. Rock (capital R)

b. Rock (lower case r)

2. If you were describing a rock, what would you say?

Through it All - TRUST

Trust Building Reminders

3. Explain the difference in Rock and rock.

4. Why was Moses making this comparison? What main point is he making to the children of Israel?

5. What do these comparisons have to do with trust? List what you learned about God from these passages that can instill trust.

6. How about you? Where are you on the trusting God scale? Are there times when you have rejected Him, turned away from Him or trusted in other things?

7. What was the question asked in verse 37?

Trust Building Reminders

8. When difficulties come your way, where is that which you have trusted in to save you if it is not God? Do you get satisfactory answers from TV talk shows, social media, friends or co-workers? Can you think of a time when you listened to the advice given you from someone who does not seek God's wisdom? What was the result?

9. What is the truth you find about God in the first two phrases of verse 39?

And so, when Moses said He is "The" Rock, he was saying God is the one and only Rock, there is no other. You can rely on, lean on and have confidence in Him. You can have a rock solid trust in God because He is the One who created you to be His very own. He is trustworthy!

Week One – Day Four

Ungodly Celebration

Read through Deuteronomy 32:5-18, 28 again and look for the specific phrases stating what Israel had done as it related to God. Make a list below and note the verse.

1. Moses identified God as the one and only Rock because the people had been worshipping idols. What was an idol to the children of Israel? Read Exodus 32:1-4

2. According to verse 6, what was the result of celebrating their idol?

Trust Building Reminders

Virginia Grounds

Trust Building Reminders

3. God created the human race to be His very own. In His commandments given on tablets to Moses, He very clearly stated, *"Thou shall have no other gods before me."* God knows us better than we know ourselves. He knew that ungodly celebration would result in ungodly deeds. Read Numbers 25:1-9. What did Israel do that led them astray?

4. What was the *final* result of their sin of idol worship according to verse 9? Ungodly celebration always reaps consequences.

APPLICATION List some things that can be idols in the lives of people today. Spend a moment thinking about the things you celebrate in your life and the time spent in that celebration. Are they an interruption to true worship of the One True God? Is there anything or anyone in your life that is unhealthy to your relationship with God?

Through it All - TRUST

5. Go back to Deuteronomy 32 and read verses 45-47. List what Moses told Israel to do about it. How do these verses apply to your own life? As you study, pay attention to the conviction of God in your heart.

If anything you study and pray about leads to an unsettled feeling or misery of heart, don't let it turn you away from study. Instead, ask God to reveal the reason for it and help you to work through it. He loves you and wants the very best for you. And if there is something in your life that is keeping you from Him, He will let you know, but more than that, He will forgive you as you turn back to Him.

Trust Building Reminders

Trust Building Reminders

Week One – Day 5

What Are Idols

Today you will revisit your study about idols. It is important to learn what God has to say about them in order to know what they are and how you are to respond. They are as real in the world now as they were in the Old Testament days. Some false religions still worship idols made of stone. But Moses' point is that God is not "a" rock. He is "The" one and only Rock in whom we can trust.

1. Look up the following verses and write what you learn about idols, about those who worship them and any application you see for today?

Old Testament:

Psalm 115:2-8

Isaiah 40:19-20

Habakkuk 2:18-19

New Testament:

1 Corinthians 8:4, 10:14, 12:2

Galatians 5:19

Colossians 3:5

1 John 5:21

Trust Building Reminders

2. What difference, if any, do you see between Old Testament idols and New Testament idols?

3. If you are a believer in Christ and came to know Him as an adult, you may have things in your past that relate to some areas of idolatry. You may have family or friends who cannot accept the changes in you that came as a result of your salvation. But we know that Godly living can bring persecution at times.

Trust Building Reminders

God knows that and provides for us a way to live in spite of it. Look at I Peter 4:1-11. With the end of all things near, as it is written in verse 7, how are you to act even in the face of persecution? See also verse 19.

4. God is your faithful creator. What did you learn today about trusting Him?

APPLICATION Now return to Deuteronomy 32:3-4. God is The Rock whose works are perfect and all His ways are just. What relationship to these verses do you find in Ephesians 2:10 and II Timothy 2:15 and how do they apply to you personally?

Through it All - TRUST

God created you for a relationship with Him. He did not create you for you to create something else to worship, but rather to worship Him. When you do, the benefit is life-changing. When you love something you create more than God, it is all about you and the pride you have in what you have created. But when you love God with your whole being as the One who created you, it's all about Him and your relationship with Him.

When life is lived all about God and a right relationship with Him, there is confidence. There is hope. There is satisfaction and fulfillment that cannot be achieved in anyone or anything else.

Yes, God intends for us to have relationships with people. There would be no point in staying on earth if that were not the case. I love my family. I love my friends. I even love people I do not know but have the opportunity to minister to. But relationships with people can be difficult. Do you know what I am talking about? The way to healthy relationships with people is to first have a healthy relationship with our Heavenly Father, to look first to Him for advice regarding your life and relationships. He is the One to worship. He is the ultimate relationship through our Savior Jesus Christ. When we put Him first, circumstances may not change – but hearts will.

Spend some time thinking about your priorities and asking God to help you put them in their proper order. He is the first and the last, the Alpha and Omega.

Trust Building Reminders

Message Notes

Week Two, Day One

Trusting When Exhausted

In your study from Week One, you saw the song of Moses as He spoke to Israel about God as The Rock – the One and Only. In your study this week you will see David's song of praise where he recounted the security and deliverance of God as he fought the same old battles over and over again.

1. Read 2 Samuel 21:15-22. What was David's physical condition according to verse 15?

2. Who was the enemy that repeatedly came against David and his men?

3. In these last chapters of 2 Samuel, we find David approaching the end of his life. War had taken a toll on his body and He was exhausted from fighting the same old enemy over and over again. Is there an old enemy that will not

---

Trust Building Reminders

The LORD is my rock, my fortress and my deliverer;
My God is my rock, in whom I take refuge.
He is my shield and the horn of my salvation, my stronghold.
Psalm 18:2

Virginia Grounds

Trust Building Reminders

leave you alone? It could be a difficult relationship you have had for years, it could be a negative emotion such as fear or anger; or it could be a spiritual battle with doubt or sin. What battle has not been eliminated from your life?

4. In David's song of praise, how did he describe God according to 2 Samuel 22: 2-3? Complete this phrase from these verses:
a. The LORD is _____ rock
b. My God is _____ rock

5. In your own words, what does David mean by this identification of God? See if 1 Samuel 23:25 and 24:2 gives you any insight?

Through it All - TRUST

6. Make a list of each identity David gave to God in 2 Samuel 22:2-3. Underline the one that most answers a need in your life right now. Explain why it is meaningful to you.

7. How many times did David use the pronoun *my*? What personal application can you see for yourself in David's identity of God my rock that strengthens your trust in Him?

Trust Building Reminders

Trust Building Reminders

Complete your study today in prayer thanking God for who He is in your life. Has He been a refuge for you in a time of trouble? Let Him know how much you appreciate His protection. Has He been a rock for you? Tell Him how thankful you are for His strength.

He is worthy of all your praise. As you continue through the week of study, think about the question from today's lesson; what battles are you still facing? Look for David's actions for being victorious over his enemy and apply those principals to your life.

Week Two – Day Two

Crying Out

1. Read 2 Samuel 22:4-7. What is the similar repeated phrase in verses 4 and 7?

2. What a simple statement; I *call* to the Lord and then I *called* to the Lord. In verse 4 David is speaking in the present tense, I *call*. In verse 7, he is speaking in the past tense; I *called*. From verse 4, write the phrase that proves David trusted God in the present.

3. From verses 5-7, what was David's past condition when he called on the Lord?

4. Where was God? And what was the result of David's cry?

Trust Building Reminders

Trust Building Reminders

5. Have you ever been in a distressed condition? What did you do about it? Did you trust God with your condition and the outcome? Why or why not?

Often we find people who act the opposite from David. Instead of trust, there is doubt that God cares or will do anything about your distressed situation. Others, who are not believers, don't think about God in the situation at all. How often do you struggle and stress over details of your life that God will save you from if you will trust Him with it instead of trying to manage it yourself?

I learned this lesson from a painful experience in my life. No matter what I did, the pain just wouldn't go away. One morning as I concluded my Bible Study time, I simply threw my hands in the air and cried out to God. I told Him this emotional pain was more than I could bear. I opened my hands and said "Lord, I give it to you. Please take it from me." In that moment, something happened. God took it away and I no longer felt the pain.

Through it All - TRUST

Trust Building Reminders

What I learned that day is that, without realizing it, I had been holding on to the circumstances without releasing control to God. What God wants for us is that we cry out to Him and release the situation to Him.

He is not only able to heal us from emotional pain, He will as we turn to Him and let go of trying to control the situation.

> APPLICATION - Is He waiting for you to release your pain and distress to Him? What is it that you are holding on to that you need to let go of?

Now is the time. David said, "In my distress, I called to the Lord and He heard my cry." God will hear your cry. Take some time this day to cry out to Jesus and release your distress, trusting that He will hear and heal. (Psalm 28:2)

Trust Building Reminders

Week Two – Day Three

David's Song

Begin your study time by reading 2 Samuel 22:8-20. In the study yesterday, you learned the importance of crying out to God. You learned that He hears when you call on Him. Today, you will look at the actions of God in answer to David's cry. For example, in verse 4, David trusted that, in the present, He is saved from His enemy as he called on the Lord.

1. Make a list of God's actions as they related to David from verses 17-20.

2. What do you learn about David from verses 21-25? (*Remember, this is at the end of David's life after he had repented and been forgiven for sins earlier in his life.*)

Trust Building Reminders

3. Why would David refer to himself as righteous? Read 1 Samuel 26:7-12, 23 for insight.

4. If you had the opportunity to heap vengeance on someone who caused you distress and was a threat to you, how would you respond?

5. Read Romans 12:17-21 and Proverbs 20:22. What does God say about revenge?

6. How does that line up with your response to those who are against you?

Trust Building Reminders

One of the most difficult situations in life to walk through is
that of someone you have loved and trusted who has turned against you, especially when their attitude stems from jealousy or something you have no control over. That was the case with David and Saul. Saul was jealous of David to the point of trying to destroy him. But because David's heart and actions were clean, he was able to say, "God has dealt with me according to my righteousness, according to the cleanness of my hands he has rewarded me."

7. Are you responsible for what someone else feels about you that causes them to seek to discredit, or harm you?

APPLICATION - How about you toward others? Is your heart clean before the Lord? Spend time praying through Psalm 51. Ask the Lord to show you anyone you are holding a grudge against and to help you forgive.

Week Two – Day Four

Help is from the LORD

Go back to 2 Samuel 22. We are looking this week at the ways David trusted God. Read verses 26-51.

1. The song of David's praise continues. What is David able to accomplish according to verses 29-30 as he trusts God?

2. In the previous verses, 26-28, who was David referring to that God helped?

One of our grandsons has completed his service as a Marine, and another is returning from deployment in the National Guard. I can't help but think of them, and other military men and women, as I read verse 30. *"With your help I can advance against the troops; with my God I can scale a wall."* What this is saying is that God gives supernatural strength to the faithful, blameless, pure and humble.

3. How does He do that? Read Habakkuk 3:19 for insight.

Trust Building Reminders

Trust Building Reminders

God gives sure-footed confidence as we trust in Him no matter the circumstances that surround us. He gives us the ability and wisdom to stand strong against temptations and evil. He is the Rock of strength, strong enough to take down David's enemy Goliath, but gentle enough to show grace through David when the opportunity arose for vengeance.

4. David began verse 50 of his song with "therefore". This word follows a long list of God's greatness shown in David's time of need. And so, therefore He did what?

5. You saw the words of Moses last week that had been written as a song. This week, David' song is concluded in your study. What did you learn about their focus from their songs?

APPLICATION - How can you apply to your own life the principal of trusting God from these two leaders?

Week Two – Day Five

According To His Word

Read 2 Samuel 23:2-5

Whether we think of ourselves as leaders or not, we are all responsible as believers in Christ to act according to His word in all areas of our lives.

1. David was a leader. In 2 Samuel 23, you can read his last words. What do you see in verses 2-5 that indicate righteousness and trust in God?

2. What is the result of one who leads in righteousness?

3. How did David know this according to verses 2-3?

Trust Building Reminders

Trust Building Reminders

In reading these verses, you may think God is speaking of David. But instead, He is speaking to, and through, David to the children of Israel. In 22:2-3, David referred to God as *my* Rock. The **strength of the Lord was very personal to him.** The verses that follow were a personal testimony of God's faithfulness to him. But in these verses of Chapter 23, David referred to God as *the* Rock of Israel. Remember, Moses told the people that God is The Rock – meaning the One and Only. And with David, we see him identifying God as being both personal (my) and for all Israel as the one and only God (the).

4. And so the message God spoke through David in verses 3-4 speaks of who and what? Read the references below and look for the common thread:

- Isaiah 9:7

- Isaiah 11:1-5

- Jeremiah 23:5-6

- Jeremiah 33:15-16

- Zechariah 9:9

Trust Building Reminders

God's message through David is prophetic. He is telling Israel that one is coming who will rule in righteousness. When David spoke of God's everlasting covenant with Him, He was reminding the people that God promised His kingdom will endure forever. (2 Samuel 7:16) And so, God the Rock of Israel, the One and Only who never changes has given promises that are rock solid and true.

5. How are they fulfilled? See Matthew 1:1, 16-17.

God made a covenant with David that was fulfilled in Jesus. He is the Righteous Branch, the Lord of Righteousness. When God makes a promise, He keeps it. You can trust Him! Give thanks to Him today that He is worthy of all praise. Write your song of testimony and praise below.

Message Notes

Message Notes

Virginia Grounds

This is what the LORD says:
'Do not be afraid or discouraged
Because of this vast number,
For the battle is not yours,
But God's.'
2 Chronicles 20:15b

Week Three – Day 1

Trusting When Threatened

We have all had occasions in our lives when we knew a battle was brewing; perhaps in the home, in the office, even at church or in our own minds and emotions. And when a battle is brewing, knowing that we have to face it head on "tomorrow" is enough to send us running backward in time hoping tomorrow won't come too quickly.

One of my favorite passages in scripture is from Second Chronicles 20. This passage gives us such clear guidance for how to respond when we feel threatened by an enemy. The enemy we face today is an unseen supernatural force, but his threats are very real. We may not be facing three armies at the same time in the physical sense, but we can certainly face three threats to our personal lives at the same time.

And so, the same principals of response we read about in 2 Chronicles 20 can be applied to our personal lives when something or someone is coming against us to destroy our integrity, our marriage, our family, our health, our career or anything else.

Trust Building Reminders

Trust Building Reminders

1. We can learn a lot from King Jehoshaphat. Read 2 Chronicles 20 and write down the threat to Israel that you find in verses 1-2.

2. What was the first thing King Jehoshaphat did according to verse 3?

3. What does it mean to "inquire of the Lord" and how can you put this into practice in your own life?

4. What threats can you think of that face our generation? Are you facing any personal threats against you?

Through it All - TRUST

Trust Building Reminders

You have read in 2 Chronicles 20:1-2 that three armies were coming against Judah at the same time. They were uniting in the cause to wipe out the Israelites. How can you relate to something of this magnitude? When I read this passage, I thought of what happened to my family years ago. Within a six month period of time, three family members were diagnosed with cancer, two months apart. Cancer was the enemy that struck my family to destroy it. Praise God the enemy was defeated, but this shows that just as the enemy came against Judah, there are still things at work to destroy our lives.

> **APPLICATION** – Can you think of other things that are destructive that come against people today? Just as the pattern of response worked in Jehoshaphat's life, it can work for you. What encouragement for action do you gain from the king's response?

5. Based on the king's response from today's passage, what advice can you give people when they tell you they are faced with threats?

Trust Building Reminders

6. What is the command from Matthew 6:33

7. What is the warning from Jeremiah 29:14?

8. What happens when people seek advice from the ungodly rather than inquiring of the Lord? Read Isaiah 8:19-22 and write your answer.

APPLICATION - As you close your lesson today, **inquire of the Lord** regarding any challenges you face. Write your prayer below.

Week Three – Day 2

Committing To the Lord

King Jehoshaphat trusted God when he was threatened by not one, not two, but three armies coming against him at the same time. His story shows us that even godly leaders can have circumstances of facing threats from the enemy. But the way he handled his threat was to completely trust and obey the Lord.

It takes strong faith and courage to face the challenges of life. But we simply cannot defeat the enemy and win any battles in our life without having a rock solid trust in our God and Savior, Jesus Christ. He makes a way when there seems to be no way. Our part in all difficulties is to follow Him, to trust Him, to go where He leads in complete obedience.

Today you will read again 2 Chronicles 20. The first thing the king did when Judah was threatened by three armies was to *inquire of the Lord*. His trust was so rock solid that he knew he could not face this threat without direction from God. And so He prayed and in his prayer, he made commitments to God.

Trust Building Reminders

Virginia Grounds

Trust Building Reminders

1. Write in list form the three things King Jehoshaphat committed to the Lord in his prayer. Make a note of the verses.

a.

b.

c.

2. What did the king say they would do when they didn't know what to do according to verse 12?

3. Have you faced a situation that you simply had no answers for and you didn't know what to do? How can verse 12 and the king's statement help you in those situations?

4. What is required of you in order to keep your eyes on the Lord during difficult situations? Micah 7:7 and Psalm 118:8-9

Trust Building Reminders

5. We often go to others for advice and trust them to take care of our circumstances, but it is God whom we are to trust with everything. Our confidence comes from keeping our eyes on Jesus. What happens when we keep our eyes on Him?
    a. Psalm 34:5

    b. Isaiah 26:3-4

    c. Psalm 105:3-4

    d. Jeremiah 6:16

    e. John 1:29

6. What happens when we stand in his presence and cry out to Him?
    a. Psalm 34:15

King Jehoshaphat made commitments to his Lord. How can you apply these same commitments to your life in a situation you may be facing right now? Write your prayer of commitment below.

Trust Building Reminders

Week Three – Day 3

God's Response

Jehoshaphat prayed a beautiful prayer when faced with difficulty. He gathered all the people together to join him in prayer. In this prayer, he acknowledged the sovereignty of God and committed to stand before Him, to cry out to Him and to keep his eyes on God in the midst of these life-threatening circumstances. To describe his prayer and commitment in a word is trust! He was saying to God, I trust you no matter what.

If destructive forces are on their way to you and you know they are coming, will you trust God with the circumstances and the result? It is not an easy thing to do. But there is so much encouragement and wisdom to be learned from Jehoshaphat's prayer and response. Plant these steps in your heart and mind to put into practice the moment you feel threatened and have that first inkling of fear:

- Turn your attention to seek the Lord
- Fast
- Pray acknowledging God's sovereignty
- Pray making your commitments to God
- Stand before Him
- Cry out to Him in your distress
- When you don't know what to do, keep your eyes on the Lord.

Through it All - TRUST

All of this equals trust. This is how you trust the Lord.

In your lesson today, you will read God's response to this kind of trust in Him. He is our Awesome God!

1. Read 2 Chronicles 20:14-19. What was the first thing God addressed according to verse 15? What promise did He make?

2. Turn to 1 Samuel 17:45, 47. David was going to fight Goliath. How was he going to fight that battle and how was he going to win.

APPLICATION - How do you fight your battles? Think about some challenge you have faced that required a fight to win. Did you trust in your ability to win the fight or did you trust God to fight for you?

Trust Building Reminders

Trust Building Reminders

3. How can knowing the faith of David and Jehoshaphat help you when you face a battle?

4. In 2 Chronicles 20:16-17, what assurance and instruction was given from the Lord?

5. What was the king's response in verses 18-19?

Close your study time today following the king's example; bow before the Lord, worship Him and praise Him with a very *loud* voice. He is your Savior. He will deliver you from whatever battles you face. Trust Him.

Week Three - Day 4

Song of Obedience

God encouraged the people of Judah by claiming the battle as His own. But He also gave instruction for them to follow. King Jehoshaphat's response was obedience. He led by example and instruction to the people.

1. When we are facing a battle, God's desire is for us to trust Him in the middle of it and through it. As the battle is approaching, He wants us to do something that testifies of our faith and trust in Him. After the King praised the Lord, he did something with the instruction he was given. Make a list of his obedient actions from verses 20-21.

Trust Building Reminders

Virginia Grounds

Trust Building Reminders

2. Do you see in his actions a testimony of his faith and trust in God? If so, how?

3. What was the song of the people saying as they went out before the army?

4. What happened as the people sang and praised the Lord? Verses 22-23

5. What did they find when they arrived at the battlefield? (*This is my favorite part of the story!*)

6. Think about their response as they marched toward the battle. What can you learn from this about how you should approach any difficulties you have to face?

Through it All - TRUST

APPLICATION - What does this teach you about the Lord in your life? What does this teach you about how your attitude and obedience can impact results?

Trust Building Reminders

7. Read Isaiah 43:1-3. What hope does this give you about your condition as you face difficulties?

8. Close your study today giving thanks to the Lord for His love which endures forever. Praise Him for the splendor of His holiness. Seek His refuge and sing praises to His name. Read Psalm 31:1-8.

Trust Building Reminders

Week Three - Day 5

Blessings of Doing What is Right

Have you ever noticed how God will put you in a place for a specific time to hear a word from Him? I never grow tired of hearing from Him through others to affirm something He may be having me do in obedience to Him. At a time when I had been working in the study of King Jehoshaphat from 2 Chronicles 20 preparing for a mission trip to El Salvador, I attended a women's ministry event. The speaker was a friend who shared a testimony about a battle her family had been facing for five years. Her message and testimony of faith and trust was from 2 Chronicles 20. She told the story you have been studying this week, and that I had been writing that very week. Neither of us knew what the other was doing. That was God speaking. That was God working in the lives of two different women at the same time with the same message to affirm that what was true in the days of Jehoshaphat is still true in the lives of people today.

And so as you close your study for the week, I want you to review what you have learned this week about how to respond when your life, and that of your family, is threatened by an invasion of attempted destruction.

Through it All - TRUST

Trust Building Reminders

What have you learned about how to thwart the enemy? How can you begin right now to incorporate these principals learned from King Jehoshaphat into your life?

Once you have reviewed the week, continue in 2 Chronicles. In the lesson today, you will learn about the blessings that come from obedience, but also receive a word of caution for use after the victory.

1. Begin by making a list of the blessings that came from Jehoshaphat's obedience. See verses 22-28.

2. The people returned to Jerusalem the same way they left. How was that?

3. How did this victory impact other nations and what was the result?

Trust Building Reminders

What a great encouragement we have in the example of King Jehoshaphat. If you are facing potentially devastating circumstances, God says face tomorrow with faith and trust in Me. You have a promise from His word that He will fight for you. But the first thing you must do in order to move forward with hope and healing is to pray, acknowledge the problem, and ask God to work in it. Then worship His Holy Name and sing praises to Him. As you praise Him, you can know that He is in the midst of your battle making a way for your tomorrow whether it be a battle of emotions or relationships or something else. He wants you to do something, face it, move forward and receive the blessings of obedience He has for you.

But I would be remiss if we concluded this week without concluding Chapter 20. There is a very important word of caution for us at the end of the chapter, because after the victory comes the temptation. After the victory, comes complacency.

4. What do you read about Jehoshaphat from verse 32?

Trust Building Reminders

5. What important piece of information do you find in verse 33 that will be a hindrance for future generations?

6. Is there something in your home or in your life that will impact your children and grandchildren in a negative way? What does the Bible say about it? Use a Bible Concordance to find scripture that addresses the issue.

7. In verses 35-37, Jehoshaphat acted contrary to God's character by aligning himself with an ungodly king. What happened as a result?

Trust Building Reminders

The victory for the people of Judah was of epic proportions. It was an *only God can do* kind of victory. The people were on such a spiritual high they returned to the city singing and rejoicing. It was truly a mountain top experience.

But often following that kind of victory, Satan finds a way to attempt to destroy what God has accomplished in our lives. And if we are not careful to lift our shield of faith against his fiery darts, we will come crashing down in despair.

We do not know how much time passed between verse 32, which tells us the king was *doing right in the sight of the Lord,* and verse 35 which tells us his *actions were out of God's will*. However, these two verses prove to us how fickle the heart can be. And if we are not careful, following a great victory, we will fall right into Satan's snare. Jehoshaphat's sin was he did not tear down the high places, the idols. And he allied himself with the ungodly.

8. What can these two sins look like in your life today?

Trust Building Reminders

9. God gave the people of Judah peace and rest following the victory. It was during the peace and rest that their hearts pulled away from God. Why do you think that is so?

APPLICATION - How can you protect your heart from becoming complacent during times of peace and rest?

It has been a great week of study, hasn't it? Close your time with a renewed commitment to stand strong and true, trusting the Lord even in the days of peace and rest. He desires your attention and heart in good times as well as those days that are difficult. Trust Him in every season of life.

Psalm 31:3 teaches us that the LORD is our Rock and Refuge. People, places, and positions may change but God does not. Our **rock solid trust** should be in the LORD only, not our circumstances.

Message Notes

Week Four – Day 1

Spiritual Rock

REVIEW

In the last three weeks, you have studied scripture identifying God as *The Rock* by Moses, as *My Rock* by David and as *Our Rock* by King Jehoshaphat for Israel. Moses led the people out of Egypt trusting in God The Rock. David fought many battles as a warrior and led the people as King, trusting in God as My Rock. He identified God as very personal to him. And Jehoshaphat encouraged the people of Israel as they went into battle by identifying God to them as Our Rock.

God is:

- The Rock
- My Rock
- Our Rock

He is solid, dependable, and does not shatter when we cast our burdens on Him.

This week, you will study about *Your Rock*, the Lord Jesus Christ. He was personal to David and the children of Israel, and He is personal to you as a believer in Christ. You read the song of Moses, the song of David

---

Trust Building Reminders

...for they drank of that spiritual Rock that followed them, and that Rock was Christ.

1 Corinthians 10:4b (NKJV)

> **Trust Building Reminders**

and the song of Jehoshaphat as a call to praise; and today you have your own personal Song of Salvation to sing.

You are now going to see that the same Rock which stood strong without being crushed under the weight of their burdens is *Your* Rock as well.

1. Read Exodus 17:1-7. How did God provide water?

2. Read 1 Corinthians 10:1-4. Paul made reference to the spiritual rock that accompanied the children of Israel in Old Testament days. Who did he say was the rock that accompanied them?

3. Paul used the rock that gushed water by God's command and Moses participation to represent the spiritual sustenance experienced in the desert through Christ. Read John 4:7-15. How is the water in this passage described?

Trust Building Reminders

4. This woman described the coming Messiah (verse 25). What was Jesus response to her in verse 26?

5. How do these verses from Exodus, 1 Corinthians and John all relate? Write your response to each verse beside the chapters listed below.
    a. Exodus
    b. I Corinthians
    c. John

6. What happens when there is no water?

7. There have been droughts across the country in years past that have caused serious damage. List everything you know that occurred because of the drought?

Trust Building Reminders

8. Drought can also occur in our bodies? What happens to the physical body when without water?

9. What happens to the heart when we are spiritually dry?

10. How can we be refreshed? Refer back to John 4:14.

11. Is your spirit dry? Do you need to take action now to prevent cracks in the foundation of your heart, to be made clean, to put out any flames of anger that can result from a dry spirit? Read the following scriptures and write how they help in seasons of spiritual drought. Make them your closing prayer today.

a. Ephesians 5:26

b. Hebrews 10:22-23

c. Acts 22:16

Week Four - Day 2

Through it All

1. Read 2 Corinthians 1:1-11. From verses 8-9, describe the conditions Paul had experienced.

2. What did Paul say was the reason for the condition? Verse 9

3. What is the promise in verse 10?

Trust Building Reminders

Trust Building Reminders

4. When you suffer hardships, can you look back when it is over and reflect on any lessons the Lord may have for you from the experience? Did you trust Him to see you through?

5. What was the result from Paul's experience? What did he learn? Verses 3-6

6. Where (or what) did he place his hope? Verse 10

Through it All - TRUST

APPLICATION - From Paul's testimony, you find four things he experienced that are listed below. Beside each one, write your own experience of a hardship. Then respond as Paul did in your closing prayer.

- a. The condition –

- b. The reason –

- c. The promise –

- d. The result -

Trust Building Reminders

Week Four - Day 3

Song of Salvation

> **Trust Building Reminders**
>
> *"The rain came down, the streams rose, and the winds blew and beat against that house; yet it did not fall, because it had its foundation on the rock."*
> Matthew 7:25

1. Read 1 Peter 2:4-12. What name do you see in verse 4?

2. Who is being described by that name? Read Acts 4:8-12

3. What does Acts 4:12 say about salvation? Write the verse.

4. According to Acts 4:1, who were Peter and John speaking to?

5. The stone the builders rejected became the capstone. They, the Jewish leaders, threw away God's choice because He wasn't their choice of completion. The purpose of the capstone of a building is to indicate that the building is finished. It is complete. Why do you think Jesus is referred to as the capstone?

6. Go back to 1 Peter 2. In verse 6, there is a different stone. How is it described?

7. The purpose of the cornerstone of a building is to determine the orientation and design of the building. It was the most significant stone in the structure as the beginning of the process. What is the result for the one who puts their trust in this cornerstone?

Trust Building Reminders

Trust Building Reminders

8. When you choose the right cornerstone, the building securely rests upon it. Upon completion, the capstone is the last stone placed. But what happens to the one who rejects this stone. See 1 Peter 2:7-8.

9. Read Ephesians 2:19-22. Who is the chief cornerstone?

10. What takes place in Him according to verses 21-22?

11. What is the purpose of the building?

As Peter used the term *rock* figuratively of Christ in 1 Peter 2:8, perhaps it was because he could relate to the name. The name Peter means rock. But that is where the comparison stops. There are two Greek words for *rock* in the New Testament as follows:

- *Petra* is a *mass of rock, a type of sure foundation. It is solid and immovable.*
- *Petros* is a *small stone or boulder that is easily moved or tossed.*

In verse 4, the living Stone is *Petra* as is Cornerstone in verse 6. These are references to Jesus, the sure foundation, solid and immovable. Peter's name comes from the word *Petros*, a small stone that is easily moved.

APPLICATION - Can you relate to Peter's name? Are you easily moved or swayed by the opinions of others? There was a time in Peter's life when he denied Christ after swearing he would die for Him. Is your foundation strong enough to keep your faith standing even in the face of adversity? It can be by trusting in The Rock, *Petra* who is Jesus.

Trust Building Reminders

Trust Building Reminders

Jesus is not only the first stone laid on the foundation of your faith, but He is the last placed upon completion. He is the Alpha and Omega, the beginning and end. When you place your trust in Him, you will not be put to shame by stumbling and falling. Trusting in Him makes you strong. He is able to carry the weight of your life without crumbling under the pressure or your burdens as your fragile human body can do. He is with you at the beginning…He will be with you at the end.

Remember, a definition of trust is to lean without falling. When you lean on Jesus, He will catch you before your face hits the ground. Don't be afraid to lean into Him.

Life *in Him* is life *with Him*. His Spirit lives in you and you are the temple built upon the Cornerstone, Jesus. He has determined the orientation and design for your life. Awesome, isn't it?

Week Four - Day 4

Tools for Rock Solid Trust

When Paul wrote the letter to the saints in Ephesus, he began by reminding them of what they had in Jesus and God the Father. These same benefits belong to believers today. They are applied to our lives, but we tend to forget or become complacent at times. And so, in order to build our trust, we can use reminders as tools to build strong faith and trust.

Watching the construction of homes being built is such a learning experience. I watched as five homes were built across the street and down the block from where I once lived. I can assure you they would not have been completed if the building crews had not picked up their tools and gotten to work. Each crew member was gifted in a different area of expertise. The homes would not have been completed without each one completing their part in the building process.

Trust Building Reminders

Trust Building Reminders

Every believer in Jesus has been gifted in a way unique to them. (Romans 12:6) Each one is to employ their gift(s) for the building up of the body of Christ – the Church. Our trust is strengthened as we pick up the tools of our faith and press on to the finish.

1. Today, you will make a list of some of the tools of faith. Begin by reading Ephesians 1:3-11. According to verse 3, what has God the Father blessed you with?

Tool #1 - **Recognize** that you are _____.

2. Adopted children are special because they were chosen. How do you see that same idea applied to you from verses 4-5?

Tool #2 – **Be thankful** that you have been _____.

3. According to verse 6, what has been freely given us?

Tool #3 – **Accept** His _____.

4. According to verse 7, what has His grace given?

>Tool #4 – **Be Confident**, you have been_____.

>Tool #5 – **Live Pure**, you have been _____.

5. From verse 8, how was His grace applied?

>Tool #6 – **Experience** His _____ that has been _____ on you.

Lavished is such a rich sounding word, isn't it? It sounds like the most expensive, thick and rich lotion you have ever generously applied all over your body. That is God's grace. The most expensive and lavish ointment God has to give, and He gives it to us freely. The cost was Jesus death on a cross. The greatest cost ever paid, and it was for you – for your sins and mine, that we can live with Him forever. God's grace to cover our sins – lavished on us generously. That's how much God loves you. That's how much He loves me; that He would give His Only Begotten Son to die in our place so we can live

Trust Building Reminders

Trust Building Reminders

forever. How can you not trust a love like that? Experience it with a heart open to receive His grace.

6. Read Ephesians 1:13. Having been included in Christ when you heard the word of truth, the gospel of your salvation and you **believed in Him**, what took place in your life according to this verse?

Tool #7 – **Trust** the _____ _____ of promise and **Look Forward** to the _____ _____.

You have been given seven tools from Ephesians 1 as trust building reminders of who you are in Christ and how much God loves you. Use these tools when your trust is weakened or shattered and anytime you have doubt. Close your lesson in a prayer of praise for all these benefits you have out of God's grace. Your prayer of praise is the most effective tool you have for building a trust that will carry you through whatever circumstances come into your life.

Week Four – Day 5

Desired Result

Trust is a conscience decision. It is not something you see, but rather a choice you make. In this last day of study, look up the word trust in a Bible concordance. Most Bibles have a concordance in the very back section. You will find more than 100 references for trust, trustworthy, trusting, etc. Look up some of these verses and find one that speaks to you in a very personal way, one that will help you to make the commitment to trust God more. Write it below, but also on an index card to carry with you. Begin memorizing the verse, claiming it in prayer as being applied to your life. I believe you will begin to sense a change in your heart and attitude as you do this.

1. Here are a few to get you started:

    a. Proverbs 3:5

    b. Isaiah 12:2

    c. Isaiah 25:9

    d. John 14:1

    e. Isaiah 26:3-4

Trust Building Reminders

Trust Building Reminders

APPLICATION - Write your verse on trust below. Why is it so meaningful to you? Consider memorizing the verse, or write on a card to carry with you.

The message of hope given through Scripture is used to strengthen our faith and trust in God when life seems hard. It gives us encouragement when we want to give in to temptation or give up on Jesus. In these last days before Jesus comes again, we must stand strong and continue to trust God with all our heart, mind, soul and strength. Carry on sweet sister in Christ.

Jesus - My Rock of Hope

In desperation and despair we strive
To rely on choices of our own
But with faith in Christ the solid Rock
We are able to walk a path never alone.

So stop your worry and let go of despair
A lifeline for you is waiting
Grab hold of trust in the solid Rock
No more fear or critical debating.

Make the choice to lean on Jesus
Trusting what you cannot see
Let go of fear, despair and selfish desire
Go forward when Jesus says *"follow Me"*.

For in Him your life is secure
The future is in His hands
So trust the Living Savior
With all your hopes and plans.

In Him is life eternal
In Him are rewards and joy
He is God's grace lavished on you
For salvation and service to employ.

◆

Virginia

Message Notes

Through it All - TRUST

Message Notes

Virginia Grounds

ABOUT THE AUTHOR

Virginia Grounds is a wife, mom and grandmother. She is also a speaker, author, Bible Teacher, former radio host, and effective communicator. Her love of God's Word and women's ministry have given her success in speaking, teaching and writing for more than 25 years where she served on the women's ministry teaching team at her church in Plano, Texas.

She served with her husband in full-time ministry for 17 years. Helping to meet the needs of hurting people through that ministry motivated her to write *Facing Fears, Quenching Flames*. Her latest book, *Rock Solid Trust* is also available on Amazon or her website.

Her sincere and transparent approach to every message inspires and equips her audience with the biblical principles needed for daily living. You can read her blogs and hear her radio broadcasts at www.majesticinspirations.com, or contact her at vgrounds@majesticinspirations.com.

Made in the USA
Columbia, SC
11 March 2019